Laura Hurley was born and raised in a small town. She was the oldest of three children. She loved school and her favorite subject was English.

From a very young age, she loved to read. Another passion of Laura's was the love for music. At the age of 12, Laura was really big on music; all she did was sing. By the age of 14, she got into writing. She sat down and jotted down her first poem. From that moment on, she has been writing poetry.

Any chance something inspired her or touched her heart, Laura made into words. Laura finally graduated high school and went on to become a caregiver. Her love and kindness for others has always been a big part of her heart. Laura still, from time to time, worked on her writing.

She always wondered if her words would ever touch others' hearts and souls. She finally mustered up the courage.

She sent her writings into publishers. In hopes for her dreams to come true, and for all to find inspiration within her words.

I'd like to dedicate this book to everyone who supported me.

Laura Hurley

Faith, Hope, and Love Inspiration

AUSTIN MACAULEY PUBLISHERS™

LONDON • CAMBRIDGE • NEW YORK • SHARJAH

Ordering Information
Quantity sales: Special discounts are available on quantity purchases by corporations, associations, and others. For details, contact the publisher at the address below.

Publisher's Cataloging-in-Publication data
Hurley, Laura
Faith, Hope, and Love Inspiration

ISBN 9781649798824 (Paperback)
ISBN 9781649798848 (ePub e-book)
ISBN 9781649798831 (Audiobook)

Library of Congress Control Number: 2023912703

www.austinmacauley.com/us

First Published 2024
Austin Macauley Publishers LLC
40 Wall Street 33rd Floor, Suite 3302
New York, NY 10005
USA

mail-usa@austinmacauley.com
+1 (646) 5125767

I want to acknowledge and give thanks to all of the employees at Austin Macaulay publishers for all their hard work to make my dreams come true.

The Spirit of an Angel

The spirit of an angel came upon her as she lay in bed. She thinks the angels came for her sister who lay beside her, feeling as weak as a blossom that blooms in the winter. The angel walks over and lets out her hand and says in soft warm words, "I have come for you." Then lifts her spirit to the heavens above

I'm Scared

I'm scared,
> Scared to say a thing.
> Scared to open my mouth
I'm scared,
> Scared of what comes next.
> So hard to help you out.
I'm scared,
> I know you love me deeply.
> I love you deeply too.
But when you get this way,
I don't know what to do.
I'm scared.

Why Me

I can't believe that you chose me. I'm so happy, happy as can be.

I never had luck in love, you see. But now my luck has changed.

> -why me-
>
> -why me-

You are my world, my heart and soul. I could never let you go.

I know you feel the same for me. You love me very deeply, deeply.

> -why me-
>
> -why me-

My Angel

My God, please help me.
My soul is gone. My heart is broken.

My life is over.
All I need is my angel back.
My angel.
Why my God, did you have to take
My angel away from me?
Please Lord with your beautiful light
Give my angel back.
I'm lost and hollow without my love.
Return my angel,
My love to me.

Confessions of My Heart

The darkness is falling,
It's starting to rain.
My heart is pounding,
The world's not the same.

A knife embedded into my chest.
From everything I must confess.
I feel breathless,
It's so hard to breathe.
Then you grasp me and hold me.
You're my light.
You're my seed.
Shallow deep breaths, I come back to see.
The one and only,
Has always been in front of me

Forbidden Love

You hold my heart within your hands.
Why do we love the ones we can't?
Why is it that our love is so strong?
It's something that I just don't understand.
My heart is breaking because
I feel we could never be.

No matter how much I want you
That's what I see.
So I should hold you in my heart.
Until the day comes.
That are forbidden love fights the battle,
And we have won.

Forever

I see forever in your eyes
And forever is what will be.
Our love will never die.
The love we share is way too strong,
Not anyone or anything can destroy.
You and I.
We will be together everlasting.
That is how it will be.
Because the love we share; you and me.
I will love you forever,
As you will me.
Forever is how we are meant to be.

How Could You

You said you would love me forever, and our love would never die.
But I caught you with that girl just last night. You tried to lie and say it's nothing.
The way you held her so tight; that was something, that was something all right.
How could you, baby?
How could you hurt me this way?
You know my life story and what I've been through.
So how could you? How could you?

Life with You

The pain I feel inside of me,
Is all because of you, you see.
All the shit you put me through.
It's hard to have a life with you.
This pain I feel will not go away.
No matter what I do or say.
You always think the worst of me,
And your trust is never there you see.
So how can we have a life together,
If jealousy is all that's there.

Me and You

Love is so sweet, tender and true.
Like the love between me and you.
Love answers your every wish.
Nothing else can compare to this.
Love makes the world go round.
And turns a frown upside down.
Love will always see it through.
At least it does for me and you.

I Wish

I wish I could help you,
When you were upset.
I want to hold you
And make you alright.

When you hurt, I hurt,
So let me help you out.
Tell me what eats at you,
Just let it all out.

Our hearts are entwined, don't you know?
So open it up and let it grow.
I wish I could help you when you're in pain.
I wish you could let me show you the way.

The One

I know I feel more for you than you do me. My heart beats so strong, it's pounding out of my chest. My stomach fills with butterflies when you are near. You wanted my pure honesty, didn't you, dear?
My body fills with tingles with every caress. Sending me floating on clouds, I must confess. People tell me it's lust; It's just infatuation. I feel that it's more; it's so much more that I'm chasing. You're honest, you're true, pure and fun. I hope you don't mind if I call you 'the one'.

Your Home

Your home,

Your home,

Where the light can always touch your face.

Your home,

Your home,

Where the angels sing amazing Grace.

Your home,

Your home,

Where your life is lifted from

everyday stress

Your home,

Your home,

We will see you again when we rest.

In memory of a loved one for the Bates family. God bless
7-15-2010.

Memories

I've fallen so low, this feeling I'm feeling. The pressure, the hold on my heart, set on fire. Couldn't be the weather that's bringing me down. Or much deeper thoughts, that keeps spinning around. Too many memories coming back to me. Too many memories of my dad, I'm not ready to see. I can't take much more as my face covers in tears.
Why can't I get over all of my fears? Let the angels bless me and stop all my tears.

Broken Heart

My heart is aching,
My world is crashing down.
I have no more faith,
I've fallen on the ground.
My soul is broken away from me.
My life is in pieces.
A world without you,
Is a world with no meaning.
I can't take no more,
My head's hitting the wall.
I can't believe it's over,
And forever's not at all.
Why did you leave me?
Thought our love was pure and true.
Together forever, no?
Now my heart's broken in two.

Follow Jesus

Jesus is our Savior, our light can you see.
He shines down on both you and me.
He shows us the good path to follow
in our hearts.
In hopes that we all do our part.
He died for our sins, not only you and me.
He died for the whole entire country.
Think about what he's done for us,
Let's follow our hearts.
And for the love of our father,
Let's all do our part.

Halloween

Halloween Halloween
What a spooky Halloween.
When the ghost and goblins
come out and scream.

You hear boo boo.
From every corner in front and behind.
The howling from the werewolves.
That sends shivers down your spine.

The witches do cackle,
As they stir on their Brew.
The eyes of the vampire,
Has you locked in your seat.

So many trick-or-treaters.
We kindly do meet.

Listen

As you sit there,
Do you not hear that sound?
The Lord is whispering, I'll gather round.
As he speaks to you.
Take it all in, hang on every word.
For he's a true friend.
He will guide you,
Help you along the way.
Give him your ear,
Don't go astray.

Pain

We've all had those times where
We feel the whole world falling apart.
There's nothing we can do.
But feel pain in our hearts.

We hope for the best and pray every day.
To find an answer,
To have the pain go away.

Belong

When the angels sing out.
You will hear their call.
There will be peace among us all.
The darkness and shadows, all float away.
They're calling you home.
Where you can feel safe.
You can sing among them if you do like.
You'll be right where you belong.
On this cold winter night.

Shadow

In the midst of the shadows
I see you standing there.
Still dark, dim figure
Without any hair.
My eyes stay wide open.
Only to see a light beaming out.
From behind a tall tree

True Christmas

In the love of a child,
You look and you see.
The laughter of snowflakes
On a white Christmas Eve.
Children are special
So special as can be.
So give them a bright Christmas.

Light up the tree.
Show them the true meaning.
Of Christmas every day.
So they will learn,
How to give more along the way.

Christmas Day

Christmas day, Christmas day
All the children want to play.
They so want to see,
What Santa brought them this day.

Christmas day, Christmas day
The children run just to see,
All of the gifts he planted under the tree.

Christmas day, Christmas day
Children are cheerful with glee.
To see all that one has gotten.
Screaming Merry Christmas to me.

Thank you, Jesus

Thank you Jesus for the blood you had shed.
Upon that cross, what a world full of dread.
So much pain you must have gone through.
It's a scary thought to put myself in your shoes.
The nails through your body as you hang there.
A thorn-filled Halo, with blood in your hair.
I want to say thank you, again and again.
Because you are my only true best friend.

Dear Lord

Dear Lord, would you help us?
Please take care of us all.
In these desperate times of troubles.
Do not let us fall.
Let us learn to love one another.
Wrapping our arms tight to embrace.
As we look upon you
Clinging to your grace.
The beauty in your light is
Where we shall be.
As long as we trust in you,
We shall be set free.
So let's help one another
Until the day you shall call.
To bringing us home
With love, after all.

Poem written with residents of
Elmcroft
God bless

Stars

Shimmer shimmer, bright is the light.
A light you can only see at night.
They sparkle and shine down on you and me.
Showing us a whole lot of history.
Several constellation, the telescope helps me to see.
What beauty the sky holds for us to see.

Wind

It comes knocking,
Knocking at your door.
Loudly it howls
I can't take it anymore.
I cover my ears to
Drown out the sound.
But there's so much shaking
Shaking all around.
I feel like I'm spinning and
I cannot break free.
The wind has really
Got a hold of me.

Daughter

This one's for you, my little darling dear.
I want to keep you safe,
But there's so much I fear.
My heart does so race when I hear you cry.
I just want to protect you all of your life.
But I know you must grow.
Becoming somebody's wife.
You will go on to have children one day.
A daughter or two
When it comes to them you will find one thing hard to do.
Letting them go to stand on their own.
Letting them go now they're grown.

Without

A world without Jesus is no world at all.
In moments of trouble,
There's no way to stand tall.
We carry our burdens
Around with us every day.
For years and years
They'll never go away.

We would die without happiness, love in our lives.
You cannot live that way and nor can I.

Voices

The numbing pain that I feel inside of me.
The voices in my head that
I wish I could set free.
The battle that I fight every day.
I just want to make everything go today.
Maybe the deep cuts will bleed it all away.
Bleed out bleed out
I hear them say.

Praise

Be glad in the Lord and rise everyday
Sing out to our Father.
Praise his Holy name.
Uphold the beauty of his light in your heart.
Shining it out,
For all amongst the dark.
Capturing their eyes,
Letting them see.
What the Lord has in store for
You and for me.

Rainbow

A field of embers I run through.
A field so wild and so true.
Full of flowers beyond thy can see.
The sky blue, the grass so green.
With every other color in between.
A distant rainbow as you
Look to the West.

Wanting to follow it wherever it rest.
Wanting to follow it to the end.
Where I may see.
Just what I was looking for.
That pot of gold for me.

My Wish for You

I wish I could teach you all that I know.

I wish I could teach you before you grow.

I wish you would know how hard life is.

I wish it'll be easier, easier on you.

I wish you never have to live in my shoes.

I wish you have everything you ever need.

I wish all these things for the love of my sons.

All three of them, because they're all mine number one.

Daddy

My heart has been ripped.
It has been torn in two.
Ever since I lost you
I looked up to you from the time
I was small.
I was your shadow, after all.
Daddy's little girl
You never let me fall.
Now you're in heaven
Watching us all

Always Stay

I feel safe and secure within your arms.
As you hold me tightly I can feel no harm.

My body yearns for you every day.
I never want you to let go, Always stay.
Our time together is very precious to me.
'Cause I know it'll be long before another
You see
So please hold me and don't let me go.
Always stay
Make me your home.

Leaves

Look at the colors fall around me.
The beautiful colors, I love what I see.
The reds, the yellows, the browns so fair.
I love how much they brighten my hair.
It's only once a year that you will see this.
Mountains of beauty and colors of Bliss.
I lay there so still, as they fall all around.
The wind carries them before they hit the
Ground

My Tiger

I feel as I'm floating on clouds above.
Floating like an angel, shown so much
Love.
You call me your queen,
Your kitten you say.
I hope this kind of love never goes away.
I know one day we'll meet.
Oh the sparkles that fill our eyes.
As you hold me in your arms,
And our tongues intertwine

Leeches

Do you not see them,
Crawling up and down?
Do you not see them,
They're all over the ground.
They slither up your leg,
Like a branch to a tree.
Slimy little creatures
Running so free.
You find them around water.
Swamps may be best.
Just stick to your skin
If you let them, I guess.
They've used them for,
Medical reasons, I dare say.
They've used them to suck all the
Bad blood away.

Meant to Be

The anger I feel deep inside of me.
Pushing me through walls,
Making it so hard to breathe.
My chest lit on fire,
Pain trembles in my heart.
You should have never said
We were to part.
I will make it through this
One day you will see.
I will be the queen,
I was meant to always be.

Risen to Fall No More

Lord, I am calling, calling on you now.
My life is in pieces. I tremble to the ground.
I need you to lift me, raise me up again.
I know you can do so you're my best friend
You help me up over again and again.
You think you'd be sick of me,
Especially by now.
Since I keep making mistakes
Hitting the ground.
You keep pulling me back,
To your light and Grace.
I looked to your eyes what a beautiful face.
I've risen I'm standing,
Only to see that this time.
You've made an angel out of me.

What I See

The shadows I see I do embrace.
Such sadness sat upon their face.
I would love to help them,
Only if I can.
People may think I'm crazy.
Because they don't understand.
They cannot see what I can see.
They cannot hear all their pleas.
You will find there's more to this life even after death.
But I guess that won't happen until you rest.

Baby Boy

God answered my prayer
When he gave me you.
It scared me so much
When you started turning blue.
My little baby boy
I feared I never would see again
As you were pulled from my arms.
I began to pray
Please God, don't take my little boy away.
Look at my life and all I have done.
Please take me instead, leave my son.

My First Born

I cannot stand the silence
Between you and I
My life is in shambles, I wish I could die.
You're my first born and it kills me inside.
I live with this pain, I hide deep down inside
I guess I'm not worth nothing to you.
The fact I gave you life,
Just does not do.
But don't worry about me
My heart will stay broken two.
I will live on and do as I do

Mama's Boy

He clung to me like glue
When he was young.
Stuck to my shoes.
Oh how much fun.
I never could step out of his sight.
If I did he would scream,
What a fright.

Now that he's grown, I miss those days.
He's out on his own making his own way.
I wish I could see him more than I do.
Whatever happened to that little boy
I once knew?

Ashes to Ashes

The fire that fuels out of your mouth.
Burning and crashing the
Whole world down.
We all try to hide from the demon inside.
We fear that we will most likely die.
Our bodies will be scattered
Amongst the ground.
Ashes to ashes
Dust all around.

Heavenly Hold

I scream and I shout, can you not hear?
My voice is trembling, I'm so full of fear.
No one will find me, not find me here.
Buried so deep in a cavern of flowstone
Rock shears.
I can't hold my breath no longer
I feel water seeping in
My lungs start collapsing before I see light
Again.
The beauty in the light, I do embrace.
For there I see such a heavenly face.
Thy Father grasps me, holding me tight.
Bringing my body fully back to life.

Kind of Love

I want that kind of love,
The love that has no end.
A love with open honesty.
No bitterness blended in.
Pleasing each other in every way.
No matter what that is.
I think I found that loving you.
Tell me is that what this is.

My Love

I love when I hear and see you my heart
Skips a beat.
I feel I can walk on rivers and the deep
Blue sea.
My body shakes and quivers with your
Passionate touch.
I can live like this forever.
With you I surely must.

Dear Joyce

The angels are singing amazing Grace and shining their light on your beautiful face. The Lord stands amongst them all, as they embrace. Reaching his arms out calling your name. You may take his hand, your family does say. Let him wrap his arms around you, freeing you from all the pain.
There will be some tear shed once you are gone. But we are crying in happiness because you've reached the beyond. We know we will see you again one gracious day. When the Lord looks upon us and takes us his way.

You will have everything ready standing there with him. All things dusted and beauty within them. Your wings will be warm as you wrap them around us. And the angels will sing in the glory that surrounds us.

In memory of Joyce Holdrege.
God bless her family. 10-29-20

Don't Cry

He was a good man.
He had a heart of gold.
He taught us everything we know.
We had our laughs, we all had our cries.
But through it all he loved us the same inside.

He was our father,
He taught us to love we know.
But now he's gone from us.
I just don't know how to let him go.

I know some people feel that
He left us behind.
But now he can be with us all the time.
He'd want us to be happy
Don't hold pain inside.
As he smiles over all of us,
And says don't cry.
Don't you cry.

Now he's in heaven with the Lord above.
We should be thankful for the laughter and love.

He was our father.
He taught us the love we know.
But now he's gone from us.
I just don't know how to let him go.

Don't cry, don't cry, don't you cry.

     In memory of David W. Hurley
     A dear beloved father. July 19 2005

www.ingramcontent.com/pod-product-compliance
Lightning Source LLC
Chambersburg PA
CBHW071248130726
47998CB00003B/1095